Animals That Help Us

Horses on Patrol

by Wiley Blevins

Red Chair Press   Egremont, Massachusetts

Look! Books are produced and published by Red Chair Press:

Red Chair Press LLC   PO Box 333   South Egremont, MA 01258-0333

www.redchairpress.com

Publisher's Cataloging-In-Publication Data

Names: Blevins, Wiley

Title: Horses on patrol / by Wiley Blevins.

Description: Egremont, Massachusetts : Red Chair Press, [2018] | Series: Look! books : Animals that help us | Interest age level: 004-007. | Includes Now You Know fact-boxes, a glossary, and resources for additional reading. | Includes index. | Summary: "You know that pets can be fun. But some dogs, horses, pigs, and more have important jobs to do. With Animals That Help Us young readers will discover how animals help us stay safe. In New York City, and many other locations, horses are a valuable part of the police department. With Horses on Patrol, readers will learn how the NYC Mounted Police Unit lives and works to keep the city safe."-- Provided by publisher.

Identifiers: ISBN 978-1-63440-319-1 (library hardcover) | ISBN 978-1-63440-367-2 (paperback) | ISBN 978-1-63440-325-2 (ebook)

Subjects: LCSH: Police horses--Juvenile literature. | Mounted police--Juvenile literature. | CYAC: Police horses. | Working animals. | Police.

Classification: LCC HV7957 .B54 2018 (print) | LCC HV7957 (ebook) | DDC 363.232 [E]--dc23

LCCN 2017947561

Photo credits: All photos by Ambar D'andrea except as follows; p. 3, 7, 17, 24: iStock; p. 18: Shutterstock

Printed in the United States of America

0718 1P CGF18

Table of Contents

An Important Job

Clip! Clop! Everyone wants to pet these horses. And they love it. But these horses have an important job. They are in New York City's Mounted Police unit.

Good to Know

Most years, the New York City Police Department has 50–60 horses on duty.

Why do the police use horses? Sitting on a horse, a police officer can see far away. That's because the officer is 9–10 feet high. He or she can easily look over the crowd for any problems.

Police Horse Jobs
- keep large crowds calm and safe
- watch traffic
- keep a lookout for people doing **crimes**

7

The police horses live in a **stable** in a fancy apartment building. Inside this stable there are 27 stalls. There is also an exercise ring, horse shower, and more. There's even a special air system. No bad smells here!

Police horses are happy and healthy. Their stalls are neat and clean. They get plenty of water and special food. A vet visits them often to make sure they stay healthy. The police officers clean and brush the horses every day.

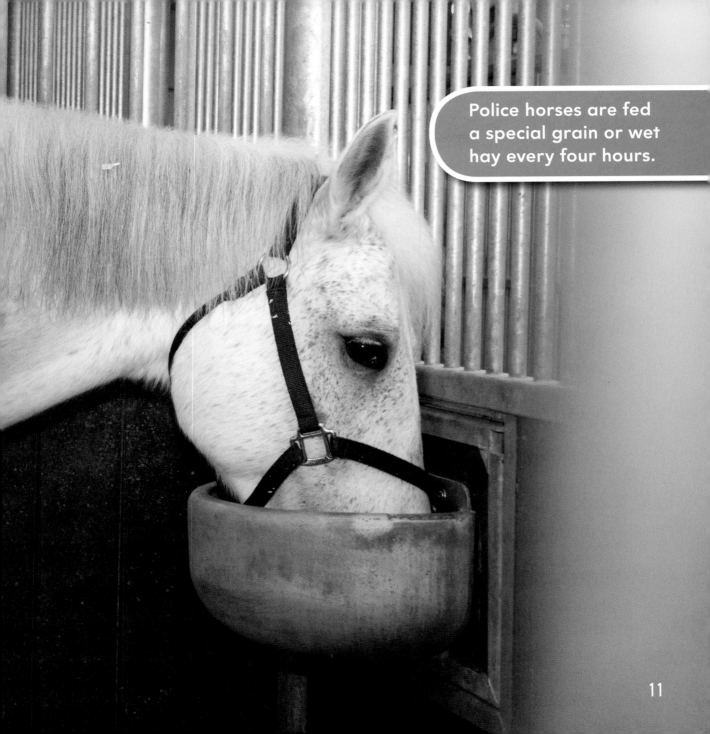

Police horses are fed a special grain or wet hay every four hours.

At the barn there's also a **farrier**. What does he do? He makes shoes for the horses. Horses wear metal shoes to protect their feet. Every four weeks they get a new pair of shoes.

The shoes are attached to the horse's hooves by small nails. But don't worry! The horse doesn't feel a thing.

Special Training

Not every horse can be a police horse. Police horses can't be afraid of large crowds. They can't get scared by sudden loud noises. They must also be friendly and strong.

Barney

Barney keeps the horses and officers company. Mice beware! The horses like having Barney around.

Police horses go through weeks of **training**. The training starts in quiet places with few people. Slowly, the horses begin working on busy, noisy streets.

Good to Know

Police horses in New York City are raised in Pennsylvania. They must be fully grown to begin police training.

Police horses must be calm with big crowds and loud noises.

The police officers also go through special training. They train 5 to 6 hours a day for three months. They learn how to ride. They learn how to care for the horses and spot health problems. They also learn how to care for the horse's equipment.

Even a little dirt on the reins could scratch the horse. Ouch!

19

Meet the Horses

Let's meet two of these special horses. This is Finbar II. He was named after an officer who died on duty. He's young and brave. But, he doesn't like loud motorcycle sounds. Can you blame him?

And this is Zeus. He has a lot of extra energy! He also loves to eat. His favorite foods are carrots and apples.

If you see Zeus or another police horse, say hello. Pet him. And thank him for his good work!

Words to Keep

crime: something that is against the law

farrier: person who puts shoes on a horse

stable: a place where horses are kept and trained

training: teaching a person or animal something new

Learn More at the Library

Books (Check out these books to learn more.)

Police Horses: Horses that Protect by Loren Spiotta-DiMare. Enslow, 2014.

Robert the Rose Horse by Joan Heilbroner, illustrated by P.D. Eastman. Random House Books for Young Readers, Classic Reissue Edition.

Working Horses by Jeanne Nagle. Gareth Stevens Publishing, 2011.

Web Sites (Ask an adult to show you these web sites.)

On-Duty with NYPD's Mounted Police
(youtube) https://www.youtube.com/watch?v=ce5AHawNqNk

HorseChannel.com
http://www.horsechannel.com/

Index

About the Author

Wiley Blevins has a lot
of respect for the police
horses in his New York
City neighborhood.
Now he knows some
of their names.